Emily Huntington Miller

From Avalon

And Other Poems

Emily Huntington Miller

From Avalon
And Other Poems

ISBN/EAN: 9783744714297

Printed in Europe, USA, Canada, Australia, Japan

Cover: Foto ©Thomas Meinert / pixelio.de

More available books at **www.hansebooks.com**

Emily Huntington Miller

From Avalon
And Other Poems

ISBN/EAN: 9783744714297

Printed in Europe, USA, Canada, Australia, Japan

Cover: Foto ©Thomas Meinert / pixelio.de

More available books at **www.hansebooks.com**

FROM AVALON

And Other Poems

BY

EMILY   HUNTINGTON   MILLER

CHICAGO
A. C. McCLURG AND COMPANY
1896

CONTENTS

5

Contents

FROM AVALON

I KNOW it well, that green and tranquil isle,
    Encircled by the arms of summer tides
That sway and smile, and whisper of the sea.
Not far away it lies ; its fragrant shades
Shot through by golden lances of the sun,
And stirred by gentle airs that wander still,
On noiseless feet, to find the chamber fair
Where, couched on mystic herbs and asphodel,
Healed of his hurts, King Arthur lies asleep.
Oft have I found its shelter.   When the stress
Of warring winds, and sharp tumultuous storms
Have left me spent and breathless on the field,
Then my swift thoughts, for healing and for rest,
Bear me away to peaceful Avalon.
The sweet enchantments of the bounteous queen
Have changed the shifting waves to fields of rye,
And seas of meadow-grass, that softly break
Against the low-browed wall that shuts about
The blessed trees, veiled in eternal bloom.

From Avalon

The bees make happy tumult, and the air
Quivers with gauzy, bright-winged, dancing motes,
And small white butterflies go shimmering by,
Silent as souls amid the scented boughs.
The skies bend low ; the pale moon idly drifts,
A phantom ship, to some celestial port,
And night and day flow on in still content,
Through blissful years in changeless Avalon.

IN APRIL

APRIL! that 's the time o' year
   When the earth is waking ;
When with every morn you see
   Signs there 's no mistaking.

When the wind is blowing south,
   And the rain's soft pelting
Sets the little brooks a-brim,
   And the last snow melting ;

When the grass begins to show
   Greener in the hollows ;
When the robin calls his mate
   And the bluebird follows ;

When the wild geese scream at night,
   To the northward hasting ;
When the maple bark is wet
   With the sweet sap wasting —

April! that 's the time o' year
   Life and love are stirring ;
Throb of heart, and leap of blood,
   Rush of soft wings whirring !

A HYMN OF ORCHARDS

UP through the wood-paths, with bird songs
 about her,
May has come softly, the beautiful child !
Skies that were joyless and sullen without her,
 Broke into sunshine above her and smiled.

Green on the uplands the wheatfields are springing,
 Cowslips are shining, and daisies are white;
Through the broad meadows the waters are singing
 Brimming with melody, flashing with light.

Ruddy with clover the orchards are growing,
 Flecked by the shadows that tremble and glide;
Round their gray trunks, when the west wind is
 blowing,
 Sways the young grass in a billowy tide.

Strong as the arms of a giant, yet tender,
 See what a treasure they lift to the sky !
Take your red roses, aflame with their splendor,
 We love the apple-trees, robin and I.

A Hymn of Orchards

Where is the lip that has worthily sung them?
   Tinted like sea-shells, or whiter than snow,
Bees, all the day, as they linger among them,
   Drowsy with nectar, are murmuring low.

Pillowed beneath them I dream as I listen,
   How the long summer above them shall shine,
Till on the boughs the ripe fruitage shall glisten,
   Tawny and golden, or redder than wine.

In the bright days of the mellow September,
   How we shall shout as we gather them in,
Hoarding their wealth for the dreary December,
   Heaping them high in the cellar and bin.

Then when the snow in the moonlight is gleaming,
   Up from the darkness the apples we'll bring,
Praising their sweets, where the firelight is beaming
   Globes of rich nectar, a poet might sing.

Tales of the vikings our lips will be telling;
   Yet, when the sagas are done, we shall say,
" Here's to the land where the summer is dwelling,
   Here's to the apple-tree, monarch of May."

IN LAVENDER

TOUCH but the yellow folds which keep
 The crumbling dust that once was bloom,
And wafts of summer sweetness creep,
 Like wandering ghosts, to haunt the room.

And straight, with dreaming eyes, I see,
 In homely garb of russet brown,
The maid whose fingers robbed the bee,
 To strew with sweets her wedding gown.

Fairer than any flower that blows,
 With bright face lifted to the day,
Led on by blessed thoughts, she goes
 Smiling along the garden way.

The lilies cluster on the stalk,
 The sucking bees make merry rout
Among the thyme, beside the walk,
 And beds with wall-flowers set about.

The sunshine fills the brooding sky,
 The birds their nesting raptures speak,
And little careless winds go by,
 With warm, light touches on her cheek.

Her apron gathered on her arm,
　Her dainty fingers gleaning slow,
She walks in youth's eternal charm,
　This little maid of long ago.

And none but those who love can guess
　What thoughts her quiet pulses stir ;
Or what dear hopes her visions bless,
　Among the beds of lavender.

PERSEPHONE

STILL the old story lives. When first I see,
  Lighting the grasses by the garden gate,
My Lady Daffodil, among her maids
Stand tall and slim, her fair head bowed in dreams,
Her yellow tresses slipping from her hood,
Mists veil the sunshine, and pale ghosts arise,
Swift, silent shades, that bear me from the day
Into the dim, sweet world where they abide.
From a low doorway, where the roses press,
A tangled thicket, to the rough gray stone,
Steps slow, with smiling eyes, a woman dear,
A little maid fast clinging to her hand.
The sound of far-off bells is in the air,
And the faint gurgle of a brook that slips,
Laughing at its own gladness, through the wall
That shuts the garden from the orchard gray.
The robins sing, the peach-tree scatters down
Her small pink shells to strew the tender grass.
The iris, with her purple blossoms, winds
In royal 'broidery along the path,
Caught here and there by knots of tulips gay,
And cool, sweet stars of snowdrops, set between

Persephone

The crowding ranks of budding daffodils —
Oh, woman dear, among the saints in Heaven !
Oh, little maid, whose feet have wandered on
Beyond the iris-path ! with each new spring
That wakes the daffodils, I walk with you
In shadowy realms, where Love with Memory dwells.

A SONG IN THE NIGHT

IN the wintry garden stood the rose-tree,
  Swaying in the tempest to and fro,
Stark and bare of all her summer leafage,
  All her life-blood frozen in its flow.

Yet, like jewels in their icy casings,
  Crowding buds were clinging, small and gray,
And a voice went singing through the darkness,
  " Sleep, my rose ! for you shall have your day.

" Brooding mists, with close warm touch, shall wake
      you
  To the kisses of the bounteous rains,
Life with faint new pulses stir within you,
  Strange, sweet thrills go trembling through your
      veins.

" All the bliss and rapture of the summer,
  All its balm and glory you shall know ;
With your soft cheek rounding into beauty,
  And your pale tints deepening into glow.   .

16

" Winds at last your scented leaves may scatter,
  Yet your heart shall hold its ripening seed.
So, perchance, in frosty autumn weather,
  From your scarlet cup a bird may feed.

" Shut within the happy round of nature,
  Flower or planet cannot fall away ;
Death is but the crown of life's completeness.
  Sleep, my rose ! for you shall have your day."

HEIMWEH

AT Naples is a garden by the sea,
  Warmed with the lavish splendor of the sun,
And filled, from wall to wall, with wanton growth
Of roses, white and crimson in their bloom.
A broken fountain spills a slender stream
Of limpid water from its crumbling brim ;
And a fair naiad, fallen from her throne,
Lies smiling, in her green nest of the grass,
At the young violets, crowding round her knee.
There, when the days are still, and glad content
Gathers her happy children to her heart,
I sit alone, to feel the healing sun
Send its warm pulses through my veins like wine,
Finding in birds, and bees, and fearless things,
That come and go along the tangled ways,
Good company, to cheer my solitude.
But when mine ear, attent to finest sounds,
Hears in the blossom-laden boughs o'erhead
The plaintive jargon of the toiling bees,
And when, through all the heavy-scented air,
The faint, pervasive breath of violets near
Steals like a dream of some remembered bliss,

Oh! then the blue sea and the bluer sky
Fade into gray, behind a mist of tears,
Through which I see our rugged orchard-trees,
Flushed with the tender beauty of the May,
Where robins build, and chide the oriole,
That in and out, among the drifted blooms,
Repeats his golden syllable of song,
Till my heart wakes with one tumultuous throb,
And, filled with longing, cries for home and thee.

AT BREAK OF DAY

OUT of a dream of music tender —
    Fairy flutes to a breathing low —
I wake to see, with its growing splendor,
    The opal heart of the morning glow.

The crystal sea of the air is flowing
    And ebbing away on its silent shores ;
The swallows ripple its coolness, going
    With the dipping of dusky wing for oars.

Webs of pearls on the meadow grasses,
    White mists trailing along the stream,
Floating up to the mountain passes,
    Vanishing slow, in a golden gleam.

I see the faint blue glint of the river :
    The fog-wreaths lift in the wak'ning breeze ;
The shadows tremble and dance and quiver,
    In changing dapples beneath the trees.

At Break of Day

I catch the scent of the locusts dropping,
  And the cinnamon roses, all a-blow ;
Of the tall red balm, where the bees are stopping,
  And the beds of the purple thyme below.

Out of the East the opal tender
  Burns, and deepens, and steals away ;
And, crowning the summer land with splendor,
  The sun comes in at the gates of day.

A HAYING SONG

OVER the meadow floats the mist,
  Rolling softly away ;
Up on the hills the sun has kissed
  Brightens the yellow day.
Faintest breath of the morning breeze,
Shakes the dew from the orchard trees,
Sways the bough where robin is saying,
"Wake ! oh, wake ! it is time for haying."

Cows are lowing, in haste to try
  Pastures moistened with dew ;
Swallows twitter, and brown bees fly,
  Scenting the blossoms new.
Meadow-larks out of sight repeat
Over and over, "Sweet ! oh, sweet !
Grass, and clover, and lilies blowing,
Round my nest like a forest growing."

Through the meadow the mowers tread
  With a sturdy stroke and true ;
And, oh for the lilies so tall and red,
  When the gleaming scythe sweeps through !

A Haying Song

Balancing over the grasses light,
Dropping with laughter out of sight,
"Ho! ho! ho!" hear the blackbird singing,
"Give me a day when scythes are swinging."

In fragrant furrows the grass is laid ;
   The golden sun climbs high.
The mowers sharpen the ringing blade,
   And glance at the western sky.
Hark the quail, with his warning call,
Whistles loud from the mossy wall ;
"Mower, whet! while the sun is shining ;
Storms may come with the day's declining."

BEFORE THE DAWN

WRAPPED in the shadows of the leafy wood
    The sweet day sleeps, while all her downy
      brood
Of fearless birds, close nestled to her breast,
In safe content within their shelter rest.

A silver film floats o'er the tranquil lake,
Lest the young morn too early come to wake,
With his light kiss, and touch of wooing grace,
The rosy flush along her dimpling face.

Then from the dusk where woods and waters meet
A little wind steals out, with noiseless feet,
Whispering, "O happy birds ! the world is new ;
With stainless skies, and balm of summer dew.

" They are all gone, those noisy, hurrying men,
Whose heavy feet tread loud on moor and fen ;
Whose hands break through your bowers, in haste to
    spy
Your woodland secrets with a curious eye.

Before the Dawn

" The thin air floats in silence rare and sweet,
For your pure harmonies again made meet ;
No jarring sound the perfect stillness breaks ;
Sing, happy birds! before the day awakes."

The little wind runs on, and one swift note
Leaps, low and glad, from some soft pulsing throat,
Yet tremulous, as if, from visions deep,
A child laughed out, and turned again to sleep.

An answering call, and then a peal of song
From a far covert ringing, full and strong ;
Then song on song, the widening chorus grows,
A flood of music, swelling as it flows.

Swift waves of melody, that break in spray
Of silver notes, tossed up, and caught away,
Till the sweet tumult slowly sinks at last
To silence, trembling with its rapture past.

AT SEA

NO moon the star-lit deeps to sound ;
　　No shore to mar the perfect round ;
With dark sails curved and prow a-light,
The ship speeds onward through the night.

The parted wave glides swiftly back,
Forever closing on our track,
And crowding pearls, an endless tide,
Slip from the furrow's curling side.

Faint tropic winds, with ghostly feet,
The shadowy deck unchallenged beat,
Flit through the dusky sails, and speak
With soft, sweet lips, against my cheek.

Deep unto deep, with listening soul
I hear a solemn cadence roll ;
Soft, rhythmic pulses, throbbing slow,
From depths above to depths below.

One full, mysterious life, whose sound
Sweeps through creation's utmost bound,
Thrills to each sobbing breath, and hears
In rippling waves the swing of spheres.

At Sea

No far-off isle of being hides
Beyond the circling of its tides ;
No barren shore but sometimes glows
With drifted bloom of summer rose.

O watchful helmsman ! if we go
To reef or port what heart can know,
Save that eternal currents keep
Their steady course through every deep.

So, lapped in happy dreams I lie,
The world, a bubble, floating by ;
The silent sky, the whispering sea,
But hollowed hands to shelter me.

IN THE GARDEN

O DUSKY bees! that murmur on in sleep,
　　Hearing the wind stir in the leaves o'erhead,
Scenting the boughs, with blossoms laden deep,
　　　　Waken! for she is dead!

Dead, in the cloistered stillness of her room,
　　Brimming with moonlight and with perfumed air;
The wandering breath of all the garden's bloom
　　　　Floating about her there.

I think the stars know, for that way she went,
　　Her white soul wafted upward, through the night,
Till its pure radiance with their glory blent,
　　　　Light vanishing in light.

All the flowers know; their waxen faces press
　　Against her cheek, unmoved by any breath;
And on her breast, in dainty loveliness,
　　　　That has no fear of death.

But you, from out your elfin land, have brought
　　For us the secret of the honeyed dew;
Since for our joy your patient skill has wrought,
　　　　Can sorrow touch you too!

In the Garden

But late she sat to mark, with smiling eyes,
  Your busy multitude make holiday ;
And said, " These fairy artisans are wise,
    Who turn their toil to play."

" They tell old tales, in Andalusian rhymes,
  And dance to tinkling zithers, as they go ;
For their fine sense can hear the blossom-chimes
    When the wind sweeps their snow."

But late ! but late ! pale shadow of delight !
  Faint, mocking echo of a music fled.
O dreaming earth ! O silent, smiling night !
  Waken ! for she is dead.

A WOMAN

"I LOVE," she said, with her faint, sweet smile,
    "But I shall not narrow this life of mine;
Or bid my spirit its thirst beguile
    With the joys that women still count divine.
Why, I am a soul! I am part of God!
    I doubt, and question, — have wings to mount;
Do you think I shall only moil and plod,
    And fill my cup at the common fount?"

That was only a year and a day —
    Last night her fingers were softly pressed
On the downy head of a babe, that lay
    With warm, wet mouth at her gracious breast.
"Do you think," she said, "there is rarer bliss
    Where the long bright cycles of heaven unroll?
Or any wonder more deep than this,
    To share with God in a human soul?"

THE MATIN MOON

OUT of the east she came ; her curving prow
    Bright with the radiance of the under-world
Where, all unseen, her golden shallop coursed
Among the stars.   Around her softly swelled
The pearly tides of morn, and, walking near,
One tranquil planet bare her company.
The cool gray east began to pulse and glow
Deep in its opal heart with rosy fires,
Slow, wavering lights, whose growing splendor swept,
A mist of gold, to dim her pale sweet ray ;
And lovely still, and lovelier as she went,
She sailed away into the brightening blue,
Freighted with dreams, that wait the evening star.

MOTHERHOOD

SWEET Mary! Mother of my Lord!
　　Through the faint light thy pictured face,
　　Touched with the glory and the grace
Born of the Angel's wondrous word,
　　Draws my eyes upward to its place.

What dost thou dream, O woman dear,
　　So late a child, whose careless feet
　　Found the green paths of girlhood sweet,
Nor guessed what rapture, drawing near,
　　Would fold thy heart in bliss complete?

They ponder much, these mother souls
　　That clasp their secret close, nor tell
　　The strange, exulting thoughts that swell,
A soundless tide, whose fulness rolls
　　To shores where blessed visions dwell.

And since that hour when first for thee
　　The hope of all the ages smiled,
　　And love and loss were reconciled,
No mother's heart but thrills to see
　　A world's redeemer in her child.

Motherhood

Sweet Mary, if some glistening wing
    Showed through the darkness, dim and pale,
    And angel voices cried, " All hail !
Lo, the swift days to thee shall bring,
    Brimmed with love's wine, life's holy grail,"

I think I should but lift mine eyes,
    And see again thy radiant face
    Shine, still and tender, from its place,
And, grown like thee, serene and wise,
    Should thank my Lord for that dear grace.

MY BEACON

I LOOKED across the bay,
   When the tide came over the bar,
And saw, through the rain, the harbor-light
   Shine like a great white star.

I trimmed my cottage lamp
   And sighed at its tiny spark,
Thinking the ships, for leagues away,
   The harbor-light could mark.

But mine — a little way
   Along the treacherous sands,
And the murky night took up the ray
   Quenched in its pitiless hands.

A keel that touched the shore,
   A carol, a footstep light,
And one stood safe at the open door,
   And there was no storm nor night.

My Beacon

"Dear heart," my lover said,
His hair with the sea-fog damp,
"Across the bar, with the rising tide,
I steered by thy guiding lamp."

Fair shone my cottage lamp;
A wonderful star to me.
For dearer my lover's wave-worn boat
Than all the ships on the sea.

HER WORLD

BEHIND them slowly sank the western world,
  Before them new horizons opened wide ;
" Yonder," he said, " old Rome and Venice wait,
  And lovely Florence by the Arno's tide."
She heard, but backward all her heart had sped,
Where the young moon sailed through the sunset red ;
" *Yonder*," she thought, " *with breathing soft and
    deep,*
My little lad lies smiling in his sleep."

They sailed where Capri dreamed upon the sea,
  And Naples slept beneath her olive-trees ;
They saw the plains where trod the gods of old,
  Pink with the flush of wild anemones.
They saw the marbles by the master wrought
To shrine the heavenly beauty of his thought.
Still rang one longing through her smiles and sighs :
" *If I could see my little lad's sweet eyes!* "

Down from her shrine the dear Madonna gazed,
  Her baby lying warm against her breast.
" What does she see ? " he whispered ; " can she
    guess
  The cruel thorns to those soft temples pressed ? "

36

" Ah, no," she said ; "she shuts him safe from
    harms,
Within the love-locked harbor of her arms.
No fear of coming fate could make me sad,
If so, to-night, I held my little lad."

" If you could choose," he said, " a royal boon,
    Like that girl dancing yonder for the king,
What gift from all her kingdom would you bid
    Obedient Fortune in her hand to bring ? "
The dancer's robe, the glittering banquet hall
Swam in a mist of tears along the wall.
" Not power," she said, *" nor riches nor delight,*
But just to kiss my little lad to-night ! "

WITHOUT

ONCE, in the twilight of a wintry day,
    One passed me silent, struggling on his way,
With head bowed low, and hands that burdens bore,
And saw not how, a little space before,

A woman watched his coming, where the light
Poured a glad welcome through a window bright,
Set thick with flowers that showed no fairer bloom
Than her sweet face, turned outward to the gloom.

Yet when his foot, with quick, impatient stride,
But touched the step, the door swung open wide ;
Soft hands reached swiftly out, with eager hold,
And drew the dear one in from storm and cold.

O love ! whose eyes, from some celestial height,
Behold me toiling, burdened through the night,
Tender of every blast at which I cower,
Yet smiling still, to know how brief the hour ;

Keeping within thy radiant, love-lit home,
Some glad surprise to whisper when I come —
'T is but a breath till I the door shall win,
And thy dear hands will swiftly draw me in.

IF I SHOULD WAKE

IF I should wake, on some soft, silent night,
 When the west wind strayed from the garden's
  bloom
To creep, with fitful touches, through the room
And see thee standing in a space of light,
Making the dusk about thee faintly bright,
With the old smile, like starlight in the gloom,
Would my heart leap to claim thee from the tomb,
Without a doubt to jar its full delight ?
Or should I wait, with longing arms stretched wide,
And know, with sudden trembling and amaze,
Some subtle change in all thy being wrought
Since thou by death wast touched and glorified ?
Then come not back, lest I should go my ways
Bereft anew of love's dear, changeless thought.

SHELTER

A SINGER by the sudden tempest blown
  Out from the summer lands of his content,
Walked 'mid the jostling multitude alone,
  And mourned his bitter fortunes as he went.

"O heart," he sighed, "whose wishes were so small,
  What didst thou ask, that thou shouldst be denied?
Only a quiet spot, where sunbeams fall,
  A little shelter in a world so wide."

A flock of startled doves rose at his feet,
  And fluttered upward through the gusty air;
Striving in vain against the blast to beat,
  To reach their nests above the belfry stair.

Then stooping to the frowning prison walls,
  They sought the grated windows, one by one;
And huddled close, with tender brooding calls,
  They smoothed their ruffled plumage in the sun.

Their fearless eyes shone soft as summer stars,
  Through purple shadows of the deepening night;
And a wan face, behind the prison bars,
  Flushed with a sudden gladness at the sight.

The Singer went his way, no more alone,
    But smiling at the sweetness of his thought :
"O heart of mine," he said, "hast thou not known
    The wisdom to thy gentle comrades taught ? "

"This is but shelter, where to-day we wait,
    Not the dear haven that we fain would see ;
Yet, to the quiet heart, a prison gate
    A peaceful covert from the storm may be.

"Some morn, it matters not if soon or late,
    Thou shalt take wing with swift exultant sweep ;
And find thy kindred and thy lost estate,
    Beyond life's prison-bars and donjon keep."

MARGARET

THROUGH the doorway shone the summer
    morning,
  Rich with bloom to tempt the honey bees ;
Small blue waves ran whispering to the sedges ;
  White sails curved to feel the eager breeze.

I remember still the loons' weird laughter,
  And the gray gulls, wheeling overhead ;
Then a low voice, full of pity, saying softly,
  " Did they tell you little Margaret was dead ? "

" Little Margaret ! — you see the daisies
  Growing knee-deep, on the windy hill,
How she loved their bonny, road-side beauty,
  She is dead, and they are blowing still."

" If a bird dropped sudden into silence,
  One, with ear attent, would miss its lay ;
Is there, anywhere, a heart of nature
  That can grieve for sweetness passed away ? "

Margaret

" You remember all her winsome beauty,
   God had made her very sweet and fair ;
Are such graces wholly lost in dying ?
   Do you think she can be sweeter over there ? "

" And if you and I should one day meet her,
   Crowned and radiant, by the river-side,
Do you think that we should surely know her
   For the self-same little Margaret who died ? "

Only tears for answer, while the thrushes
   Filled the leafy covert with their glee ;
Idle butterflies went drifting past us,
   Golden blossoms, blown along the lea.

In its green cup lay the shining water,
   All its blue waves blossomed into spray ;
On the hill the crowding ranks of daisies
   Swayed like white-robed children at their play.

Through the doorway shone the summer morning,
   Not a tint of all its freshness fled ;
Only we two, sitting in our silence,
   Mourned that little Margaret was dead.

THE WELL OF PRAISE

I

HASSAN the Just within his garden-bound
  Sat where the fountain made a pleasant sound ;

The white roofs glistened in the noontide heat,
The air in tropic pulses fiercely beat ;

But glossy limes and thick pomegranates made
Within the garden-walls a grateful shade,

And the broad pavement by the fountain's brim,
Beneath its clustered palms, lay cool and dim.

A carpet from the looms of fair Cathay —
A flowery splendor — on the marble lay,

And near at hand, companion of his rest,
Wrought like a serpent, with a jewelled crest,

His favorite pipe, whose cloudy odors seemed
The subtle spirit of a mystic dream.

Tall flagons held the cool and sparkling draught
Of harmless nectar, by the prophet quaffed ;

And crystal vases, heaped with purple grapes,
Through silver network showed their graceful shapes.

Near by a holy man, with reverent look,
Read in the pages of an ancient book ;

And ever and anon, as Hassan heard,
He murmured to the oft-repeated word

" Allah il Allah ! " and with forehead raised
Toward the holy place devoutly gazed.

" Father," at length he said, " of gold and store
Allah hath given me till I crave no more ;

" Seven goodly sons around my table stand,
And one fair daughter, pearl of all the land ;

" An upright walk hath wrought me love and fame —
Hassan the Just the people call my name ;

" Therefore, that Allah may have fitting praise,
A mosque within my garden will I raise ;

" So may the thanks I offer day by day
Join with the prayers that true believers say."

" Son," said the holy man, " for praise and prayer
The faithful find their temples everywhere,

" And not alone from sacred mosque uprise
The words that reach the gates of Paradise.

" But wouldst thou teach to many a scoffing tongue
The song of praise it never yet has sung,

" Bid in the desert sands a fountain burst,
Whose cooling drops may stay the wanderer's thirst."

II

Hassan the Just from out his treasures told
A camel's burden of the yellow gold,

And patient men beneath the master's eye,
Digged for the spring whose fountains never dry,

Until, at length, it cleft the rock and lay
A living jewel, in the eye of day.

They built it round about on every hand
With solid stone, against the drifting sand,

And cunning workmen from the palace came
And carved on every stone the holy name.

An hundred camels from the fruitful Nile
Brought the fat earth that makes the desert smile,

And Hassan planted, when the work was done,
Seven goodly palm-trees — one for every son ;

So where the hungry waste before was seen
The Well of Praise stood ringed in living green.

III

Still o'er the track whose ghastly landmarks lie
In whitening bones beneath the traveller's eye

Creeps with slow pace the caravan that bears
Spices and myrrh and rich Arabian wares ;

And still the fountain draws its rich supply
From the cool depths, unseen by human eye,

And green and fair, as in the ancient days,
The palm-trees stand about the Well of Praise.

The swarthy merchant lifts his longing eyes
To see from far the slender columns rise ;

And while the thirsty camels, kneeling, drink,
Their master reads upon the fountain's brink,

Ere to his lip the precious draught he brings :
" Allah is great, who gave the water-springs."

LOVE AND LIFE

LOVE chose a face clear-lighted by the soul,
   And wrote on cheek and brow her thoughts
      divine :
" The stars shall vanish from the heaven's wide scroll,
Time's story end — eternity is mine."

Life came, and, at her bidding, pain and care
   Blurred the fair page, its rosy hues effaced,
Hiding the tender story written there
   With heavy lines, by ruthless fingers traced.

Death came, and breathed upon each crossing line
   Till, sunk in frost, it paled and vanished slow ;
And lo ! once more Love's prophecy divine
   From the scarred brow shone forth with heavenly
      glow.

And when men looked upon the coffined face,
   They said, " He lies as in a dream of bliss ;
Such calm he wore in manhood's early grace ;
   So smiled his lips when youth and hope were
      his."

48

Love and Life

Under the down-dropped lids there strangely crept
  Serener light than falls from star or sun,
And a glad whisper through the silence swept,
  " Time's story ends when Love's is but begun."

MY SAINT

THIS is her picture, framed about
    With palms and shadowing wings,
Set in a softly curtained niche,
    Apart from common things.

And though her hand no lily clasps,
    Her brow no aureole wears,
She is my saint, whose steadfast eyes
    Turn all my thoughts to prayers.

She walked, as in a cloister's shade,
    Along life's dusty way,
And rosaries of blessed deeds
    Slipped through her hands all day.

The incense of her prayers arose
    Before a household shrine,
And common mercies to her taste
    Seemed hallowed bread and wine.

The sprinkling of her pitying tears
    On sinful souls was shed ;
Her heavenly patience was the ban
    From which all evil fled.

My Saint

For serge and ashen weeds she wore
  The shining robes of love ;
The angels keep her sisterhood
  In calendars above.

IN SICKNESS

SING to me, tender voice; for when I sleep
My soul goes drifting o'er a shadow deep
Whose ghostly islands, in its tides set low,
Sink and dissolve like snow.

No friendly ships on cheerful errands haste
To bear me company across that waste,
But through the cold gray hollows of the deep
My lonely course I keep.

Somewhere beyond, I think, lies blessed land,
But, tired and bruised, I cannot reach the strand ;
A tossing boat, whose sailor lieth pale,
Wrapped in his useless sail.

From those chill shades this pleasant world of ours,
With winds, and stars, and 'broidery of flowers,
With pomp of summer noons, and morns of May,
Seems dim and far away.

Sing to me, tender voice, that as I go
The music of thy song may follow slow ;
A silver cord to moor me to thy shore
Lest I come back no more.

JUST TO FORGIVE

NOT a hard master did I deem my Lord,
But just, since he had pledged his kingly word,
And written in the changeless rolls on high,
"The soul that sinneth, it shall surely die."

So when, in dreams, I heard the solemn call
Summon my spirit to the judgment hall,
Trembling I cried, "In this my utmost need
Still with his Justice let his Mercy plead."

Lo, to the door, with greeting hands, there came
One with a welcome in my Lord's dear name.
Grasping her garment's hem, I poured my plea,
"Oh, tender Mercy! let me come with thee!"

"Justice must smite," — but, with a radiant look,
She showed the pages of the judgment-book;
"I am his Justice; hast thou never heard
'Just to forgive' is written in his word?"

ANOINTED EYES

THEY brought it from the quarry, where it slept, —
    A block of marble without flaw or stain, —
   And all the jostling crowd, intent on gain,
Praised it for whiteness, like the snows, wind-swept,
In cold blue hollows from the sunlight kept.

There, to its side, two friends in converse came :
    One was a sculptor, with a hand made wise
   To shape immortal dreams for mortal eyes,
And one a poet, with a soul whose flame
Was fed by sorrow that no lip might name.

One said : "O marvel! wrought for man's delight
    By the kind gods, from some most precious clay,
   I see thy snows, dissolving, slip away
From lovely shapes of angels, strong and bright,
Their buoyant robes upborne by pulsing light."

The other, musing, answered : " As they go
    In wide procession through the heavenly space,
   One, looking westward, veils her radiant face ;
Yet by my soul's full, swelling tides, that flow
Beneath her faint, sweet light, my Love I know."

LIFE'S PARABLE

ASHES for beauty ! all her hair's bright gold,
 Her red mouth curving to the heart's light mirth,
Her lilied brow, her cheek of loveliest mould,
 Ashes for beauty ! 't is the doom of earth.

But lo, the wild rose stretched her arms to reach
 The low, green mound, with tender grasses rife,
And my heart read the lesson of her speech,
 " Beauty for ashes ! 't is the gift of life."

IN HIS KINGDOM

A SOUL set free came trembling through the night
And stood, all naked, in the judgment-light.

" Alas," she cried, " so pressed with life was I,
No space I found to teach me how to die.

" Unshriven I came ; — I was so full of care
No time had I for penance or for prayer.

" I dwelt where men were in such evil case
Their woful eyes still held me to my place.

" Nor did I heed my garments' fret and stain,
If so I might a little ease their pain.

" And scarce my thought from haunting care could stay
To say at morn, ' Ah, Lord ! another day.'

" But flying still, and followed hard by fear,
I loved and toiled, and waked to find me here ! "

Then round the naked soul the judgment-light
Grew, like a lily's bloom, to garments white ;

In His Kingdom

And a new dawn of rapture and surprise
Shone through the doubt and sorrow of her eyes,

As a voice whispered, "Since thou didst not fear
To drink my cup on earth, come share it here!"

And gazing on a face, unknown till now,
She cried, exulting, "Master! is it Thou?"

IN PORT

SEPTEMBER 7, 1892

"I know not where his islands lift
Their fronded palms in air,
I only know I cannot drift
Beyond his love and care."

ANXIOUS and spent, and doubtful of the helm,
    And beating slow across a waste of sea,
Often, athwart our track, there dropped a bark
Moving straight on before some heavenly wind
That filled the sails and fanned the helmsman's brow.
Sometimes, on tranquil morns, we heard his song,
Serene and sweet, yet throbbing with a note
That shook the heart, for still he sang of home.
Sometimes we hailed him, ere he passed from sight.
"Sailor!" we cried, "tell us where lies thy port!"
And still came back the answer, clear and strong:
"I know not where, yet am I homeward bound.
This is His sea; its pulses rise and fall
As His breath moves them, and its currents set
Steady and deep, to bear me where He will."

So he sailed on ; and once, when stars were large
And luminous, through changeful purple mists,
Rocked by slow waves that bore him from our sight,
And calm with peace that lay too deep for smiles,
He drifted gently to a palm-girt shore,
And knew, at last, where God's fair islands lie.

"FALLEN ON SLEEP"

NOVEMBER 4, 1895

A TRAIL of mist on the low gray deep,
  A blur of rain on the land,
And the breath of flowers where he lies asleep,
  With one white rose in his hand.

The strong, sweet singer, who laid aside
  His lute till the dawn should come,
But drifted away with the morning tide,
  And left it forever dumb.

And what are the wonders his eyes have seen,
  And what are the secrets he knows,
He never will tell as he lies serene,
  Just clasping the sweet, white rose.

But not in the splendor of seraphs he seems,
  This child-hearted poet we knew,
In some happy garden of blossoms and dreams
  He wanders with Little Boy Blue.

"*Fallen on Sleep*"

They smile at the toys that they left for a night,
  The playthings of youth and of age,
For the man is a child in the kingdom of light,
  And the child is as wise as the sage.

And whatever marvels in dying may be,
  This lover, so tender and true,
Will turn from the raptures of angels to see
  The face of his Little Boy Blue.

AT THE KING'S GATE

MORNING by morning to his gates I came,
        Taking my portion from his liberal store,
Glad of my crumbs, and asking for no more.
Scarcely my lips their stammering thanks could frame ;
For what was I that I should think to claim
Such audience from the King, whose good ran o'er
To fill each empty soul that sought his door,
And with the blessing spake no word of blame ?
But if, some morn, his angel guards had cried :
" The King hath nothing for thy needs to-day,
Since from thy desert life no flowers unfold,
And all thy fields lie barren, far and wide,"
I should have said, and humbly gone my way :
" He is the King, to give or to withhold."

Swift from the shining presence entered One
With spotless robes, of pearl and lilies wrought.
I know not if he spake, or if the thought
Grew in his smile, as blossoms in the sun :
" Why shouldst thou come, O child, as beggars come,
Who take the gift but count the love for naught ?

This is thy Father's house.   For thee he sought,
Waiting thy coming till the day was done.
He careth for thee.   Ask for large supplies,
Put on the robe and ring, and cast away
Thy garments stained with tears, with sin defiled ;
And if his wisdom all thy prayer denies,
Secure in love, look up and trusting say :
' He is the King, yet am I still his child.' "

BENEDICITE!

TOWARDS the saffron gates of sunset
  Goes the sweet day ;
Slowly the crimson flushing of her footsteps
  Fades from the hills away.

Home from the ruddy fields of clover
  Troop the wild bees,
And small birds brood beneath the leafy shadows
  Among the orchard trees.

Behind the westward-looking mountains
  Sinks the red sun,
And voices wander through the twilight saying,
  "Peace ! peace ! the day is done."

Oh, weary day ! take hence thy burdens,
  Thy haunting care ;
We would commune alone with our hearts' treasures,
  And tell them o'er in prayer.

God bless you all, O well-beloved !
  He knoweth best
To heal your losses with his great consolings,
  And give his children rest.

Benedicite !

Soon shall this little life be ended,
  And that begun,
And angels chant above your quiet sleeping,
  " Peace ! peace ! the day is done."

.

JUDGMENT

HE said, when, on that solemn day of days,
  With sudden flame the darkened skies were
    cleft,
Two should be busy at their household ways,
  And one be taken and the other left.

Always with fear and bated breath I thought
  Of those two women, grinding at the stone, —
One to the King's bright presence swiftly caught,
  And one left trembling in the murk alone.

But now I know that judgment trumps may sound,
  And some be called, and some be left alone,
And the dull world keep on its daily round,
  Nor ever guess the King has claimed his own.

For now I know that, when the King draws near,
  Only his own with conscious gladness thrill ;
Only his own the angel's summons hear,
  Above the ceaseless clangor of the mill.

HEPATICA

THROUGH the hushed bosom of the Mother
    Earth,
Brooding her darlings in the dreamless night,
Stole with slow beat, faint pulses of delight,
The throb of life impatient for its birth,
The stir of wings eager to try their worth,
    And, with soft flutter of their garments bright,
    Her laughing babes crept outward to the light,
Wide-eyed and wondering at the wintry dearth.
    The rough winds tossed the dead leaves at their feet,
    The melting snows in the moist hollows lay,
    And overhead stretched grim the cheerless skies.
Yet in their fragile beauty, brave and sweet,
They smiled upon the changeful April day,
And made a spring-time with their fearless eyes.

ON ARACHNE'S STAIR

ON the yellow grasses, I,
  Lapped in blissful dreaming, lie.
    Above my head
    With white sails spread,
The thistle's fleet, by light winds sped,
    Floats gayly by.

What enchanted highways run
'Twixt my vision and the sun!
    Arachne's stair,
    A pathway rare,
For Fancy's vagrant feet to share,
    Dull care to shun.

Silver threads that wavering fly,
Floating upward to the sky,
    Lead through the air,
    She knows not where,
But mounts to see what pleasance fair
    Beyond may lie.

On Arachne's Stair

Heart, forego thy useless thrift!
Up the stairway follow swift!
    Perchance thy feet
    May find some sweet,
Low shore where tides in music beat,
    And blossoms drift.

Hand in hand with breezes gay,
Speed, my happy thoughts, away!
    And bring to me
    Some note of glee,
From tuneful pipes of Arcady,
    Or shepherd's lay.

THE HOUSE OF LOVE

IT stood with windows open to the light,
  And all the winds ran laughing through its halls.
Set in such splendor, on the world's fair height,
  It seemed a temple, built with jasper walls.
Of sun and moon its dwellers had no need,
  Like the fair bride, Jerusalem above,
And on its portals he who ran might read
  This blessed legend writ, — *" The House of Love."*

Once in the dawning of a summer day
  Death's glorious angel paused beside the door,
And spake no word, but, as he went his way,
  There came a sound of waves along a shore,
And Love, with fearless eyes that gazed afar,
  Arose and followed to that mystery,
Filling the dusk with radiance like a star
  That shines through purple mists across the sea.

Since then, the door stands wide : the sunshine falls
  Where last his feet across the threshold trod ;
And wafts of sweetness fill the silent halls,
  From little smiling flowers that light the sod.

Some night or morn my listening soul will hear
  ’ The old familiar footfall on the stone,
And cry, "O Wanderer! forever dear,
  I feared not, quailed not; art thou not mine own?"

A RUIN

JUST here it stood : from noise afar,
  Set on the green hill's sheltered side,
The rifted earth still keeps the scar,
  Healed by the turf, but deep and wide.

Here was the narrow path that led,
  Bordered with posies, to the door,
When swaying tulips, gold and red,
  Flamed in the tall rank grass before.

This was the door-step, rough and gray,
  Deep sunken in the weedy sod,
Where blessed feet for many a day
  On household errands lightly trod.

Here rose the chimney's blue-wreathed mouth
  Above the low roof's mossy slope ;
And here a window, looking south,
  Shone through the night, a star of hope.

Here was the garden's goodly show,
  Gay marigolds, and purple stocks,
Pinks and sweet-williams, all a-blow,
  And ranks of silken hollyhocks.

A Ruin

Still from the plum-tree's boughs the breeze
    Shakes down in May the fragrant snow,
And flowers that tempt the gossip bees
    Light the green jungle with their glow.

Still the sweet wind of summer brings
    The scent of clover from the lea,
And still the robin builds, and sings
    His matins from the maple-tree.

Ah ! dearer nest, so rift and torn,
    What art could build your walls anew ?
Or fill the dewy summer morn
    With the old music that you knew ?

The skies above you keep no track
    Of vanished wings, that soared and fled ;
And only memory's feet come back,
    Among her ruined shrines to tread.

BLOSSOM·TIME

ONE were a miracle for which to rear
    A temple where a white-robed priest might say,
"Lo, the creative spirit moves to-day,
And at his touch fair shapes of life appear;"
    Yet this soft changeful beauty, year by year,
Poured from the lavish bosom of the May,
    Decks the brown meadows, and the orchards gray,
And we but smile to note the spring is here.
    Delicate odors to the warm air cling,
And fine, tumultuous sounds of bees that speak,
    In elfin tongues, of Hybla's honeyed stream;
The busy oriole cannot wait to sing,
    But tosses upward from his restless beak
Bubbles of music, breaking as they gleam.

THE THROSTLE'S NOTE

WHEN evening shades were falling,
   I heard the throstle calling,
     And fluting to his dear
     In some green thicket near,
As if his voice, by love's own rapture taught,
From my dear maid its ecstasy had caught.

   When morning bells were ringing,
   I heard my Sylvia singing
     A-down her garden way,
     With pinks and posies gay ;
And in her song my listening heart could hear
The throstle's note, a-fluting to his dear.

THE END.

TALES FROM THE ÆGEAN.

By DEMETRIOS BIKÉLAS.

Translated by Leonard Eckstein Opdycke. With an Introduction by Henry Alonzo Huntington.

16mo, 258 pages. Price, $1.00.

The tales in this volume have a special value in that they reflect the Greek life, thought, and feeling of to-day. They have, moreover, a universal interest for their merit as works of literary art. They are simple, pure, and elevating. Though tinged now and then with melancholy, their melancholy is of the kind that, instead of depressing, buoys up and elevates the reader. — *Commercial Gazette*, Cincinnati.

This dainty little book is composed of several tales based upon the life and customs of the inhabitants of the Ægeau. It opens up a new and attractive field of interest, made all the more fascinating by the strength and vividness of the sketches, and the reality and truth portrayed in the characters, which the translator has carefully preserved throughout. — *Public Opinion.*

Each tale is dramatic, and has as distinct a plot as is compatible with short limits. There is no moralizing; the author is too eager to tell his story to stop for that. The book should find a wide welcome because of its novelty and high literary merit. It is admirably translated. — *Literary World*, Boston.

The stories are delightfully told; humor and pathos in turn call forth our admiration; and we owe our thanks to the publishers for having introduced this new author to the English reading public. — *The Boston Times.*

The stories are fresh and striking, simple in style, elemental in their sympathetic appeal. — *Independent*, New York.

The author portrays Greek life as it is with true poetic realism, and depicts the defects as well as the racial virtues of his countrymen. His stories are like so many dainty water-colors, — almost luminous in feeling, and possessing the indefinable attribute called "atmosphere." — *Beacon*, Boston.

Sold by all booksellers, or mailed, on receipt of price, by

A. C. McClurg & Co., Publishers,

Cor. Wabash Ave. and Madison St., Chicago.

THE PRICE OF PEACE.

A Story of the Times of Abab, King of Israel.

By A. W. ACKERMAN.

12mo, 390 pages. Price, $1.25.

It throws valuable light upon an eventful period of the history of this wonderful people, and presents a carefully drawn and lifelike picture of a biblical character too little known, — the courageous prophet Micaiah. As a love story it is a gem, and its historical value is marked. — *Boston Advertiser*.

The author has written a religious narrative of more than ordinary interest. The period is the most picturesque in the history of the ancient Jewish people. — *Sun*, Baltimore.

It is a vivid and thrilling picture of that wild and distant time, and deepens the interest of the reader in the Bible narrative, while in no way warring against his reverence toward it. — *Literary World*, Boston.

The stirring events in the time of Ahab have been well wrought together in this book. Micaiah is the hero; Obadiah is skilfully presented, and Elijah appears at intervals. We regard this as an excellent work, alike as a story, a study in character, and a picture of the time. — *Sunday Journal*, New York.

The descriptions of the region are good, the different scenes well depicted and lifelike, and the lessons inculcated are helpful and natural. — *Public Opinion*, Washington.

In the "Price of Peace" we have a new presentation of the character of Micaiah, who is the hero of Mr. Ackerman's romance. The Bible gives us only a meagre glimpse of the man ; here we learn to know him as a man of passions like unto our own, but wiser and greater than his fellows. The author introduces us to a period of rare interest, and we learn much of Elijah, Jehoshaphat, and King Ahab. More than all, our interest is awakened in the lovely Ruth, and we close the book regretfully in the thought of leaving her and the hills of Zebulon. — *Evening Bulletin*, Philadelphia.

Sold by all booksellers, or mailed, on receipt of price, by

A. C. McClurg & Co., Publishers,

Cor. Wabash Ave. and Madison St., Chicago.

THE CRUCIFIXION OF PHILIP STRONG.

By CHARLES M. SHELDON.

12mo, 267 pages.   Price, $1.00.

The hero is an honest, forceful minister, who believes that he should not allow his church to be simply a social club.   His efforts to stem the tide of luxury and of selfishness are told in a way that will hold the reader interested to the end. — *Chronicle Telegraph*, Pittsburg.

It is more than a well-written and well-conceived story; it is a gospel, or, rather, the gospel of Christ presented in living form, coming in contact with human life, in all its phases and with the great problems that to-day agitate the mind of society. . . . If this powerful presentation of truth in story form does not produce a profound impression on the reading public, we shall be greatly disappointed. — *Lutheran Evangelist*, Dayton, Ohio.

The story is one of intense vigor and pathos.   It will secure a very wide reading, and it should make a deep impression upon every reader and produce lasting fruit. — *The Congregationalist*, Boston.

An original and realistic story, both interesting and suggestive of earnest thought. — *The Beacon*, Boston.

The story is often pathetic, sometimes dramatic, and always convincing. It is wholesome reading to all, and instructive to those who are led to wrongly believe that the church and its pastors do not make sacrifices for, and are not in sympathy with, the poor of the world. — *Chicago Record*.

The book abounds in powerful and convincing arguments for righteousness and truth, and the young preacher with the lofty ideals, though a pathetic figure in his loneliness, commands respect for his self-forgetfulness in a noble cause. — *Literary World*, Boston.

A fine piece of realistic writing.   The duty of the Christian and the Christian minister is clearly unfolded. — *Herald*, Chicago.

Sold by all booksellers, or mailed, on receipt of price, by

A. C. McClurg & Co., Publishers,

Cor. Wabash Ave. and Madison St., Chicago.

BEATRICE OF BAYOU TÊCHE.

By ALICE ILGENFRITZ JONES.

12mo, 386 pages.   Price, $1.25.

A capital story, full of vigor and subtle knowledge of human nature; and it is as vivid and picturesque as the Bayou. — *Octave Thanet.*

The author writes with an attractive, graceful style, and with a keenness of observation which holds the reader's attention. This love story is vigorously told; the heroine is a girl with a strong sense of her moral responsibility, and the ethical tone of the story is very high. — *Boston Journal.*

Mrs. Jones's writing is marked by gracefulness and by considerable strength. Her descriptions, both of persons and of scenery, are uniformly good and often fine. . . . Take it all in all, it is one of the best of stories. — *State Register*, Davenport.

The story is very well written, and is entertaining, though inevitably sad. There is nothing exaggerated in it; and the kindly spirit which often existed in the South between master or mistress and the slave is very well represented by the family to which Beatrice and her old grandmother belonged. — *The Beacon*, Boston.

A wonderfully touching and pathetic story is that of Beatrice. It appeals to one's sympathies, while it arouses admiration for the purity and sweetness of its tone. It is full of interest, too, and while its prevailing tone is pathetic, it is not at all lugubrious. It is in every way a bright and delightful work of fiction. — *Journal*, Milwaukee.

The writer has plunged into some of the omnipresent racial problems in Louisiana society, and portrays graphically the miseries of a clever and charming girl whose blood has the African taint. — *Review of Reviews.*

It is more than ordinarily well written, full of fanciful turns of phrase and short, charming pen pastels, and would be agreeable reading even were the story a less pulse-quickening one. The author's style is characterized by a quaint and delicate humor. — *Commercial Advertiser*, New York.

Sold by all booksellers, or mailed, on receipt of price, by

A. C. McClurg & Co., Publishers,

Cor. Wabash Ave. and Madison St., Chicago.